21st
Century
Skills Library

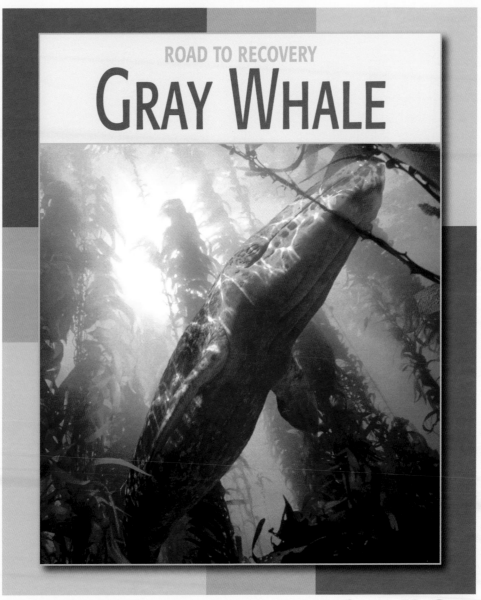

ROAD TO RECOVERY

GRAY WHALE

Susan H. Gray

Cherry Lake Publishing
Ann Arbor, Michigan

CHERRY LAKE
Publishing

Published in the United States of America by Cherry Lake Publishing
Ann Arbor, MI
www.cherrylakepublishing.com

Content Adviser: Kim Shelden, Marine Biologist, National Marine Mammal Laboratory,
National Oceanic & Atmospheric Administration) NOAA Fisheries, Seattle, Washington

Photo Credits: Cover and page 1, © Richard Herrmann/SeaPics.com; page 4, Kevin
Schaefer/Corbis; page 5, Christopher Swann/Photo Researchers, Inc.; page 6, © Nik
Wheeler/Corbis; page 7, © Natalie Forbes/Corbis; pages 8 and 12, © George D. Lepp/
Corbis; pages 10 and 14, Francois Gohier/Photo Researchers, Inc.; page 16, George
Bernard/Photo Researchers, Inc.; pages 19 and 26, © Stephen Frink/Corbis; page 21,
© Galen Rowell/Corbis; page 22, © Vince Streano/Corbis; page 24, © Roman Poderni/
R.P.G./Corbis Sygma; page 25, Bryan & Cherry Alexander/Photo Researchers, Inc.

Map by XNR Productions, Inc.

Library of Congress Cataloging-in-Publication Data
Gray, Susan Heinrichs.
  Gray whale / by Susan H. Gray.
    p. cm. — (Road to recovery)
  ISBN-13: 978-1-60279-036-0 (hardcover)
  ISBN-10: 1-60279-036-1 (hardcover)
  1. Gray whale. I. Title. II. Series.
  QL737.C425G727 2007
  599.5—dc22   2007004468

*Cherry Lake Publishing would like to acknowledge the work of
The Partnership for 21st Century Skills.
Please visit www.21stcenturyskills.org for more information.*

TABLE OF CONTENTS

CHAPTER ONE

MUD, MUCK, AND MUNCHIES

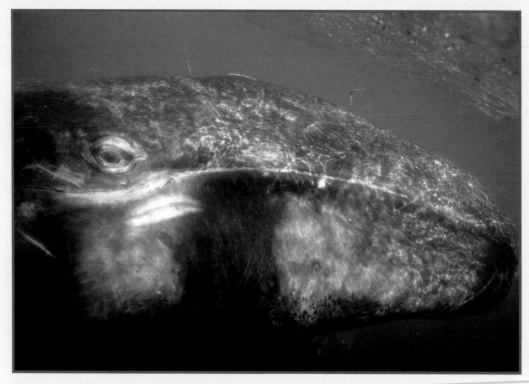

Gray whales are slow swimmers that scoop up food and mud with the side of their mouths. They eat mostly shellfish.

The gray whale takes a deep breath and dives to the seafloor. He swims along the bottom, nosing through the silt and mud. Suddenly, he rolls over on his side and opens his mouth.

Sand, worms, shrimp, and a couple of fish wash in. The whale

swishes his tongue through the muck. Water and sand gush out through

filters in his mouth.

The fish, shrimp, and

worms stay behind.

The whale swallows

and rolls upright. Then

he swims through

the cloudy water and

back to the surface.

*A gray whale in the North Pacific Ocean
surfaces after feeding from the seafloor.*

CHAPTER TWO

THE LIFE OF THE GRAY WHALE

Gray whales live in the Pacific Ocean. There are two populations. One

group lives near Korea, Japan, and Russia. The other group lives near

North America's west coast.

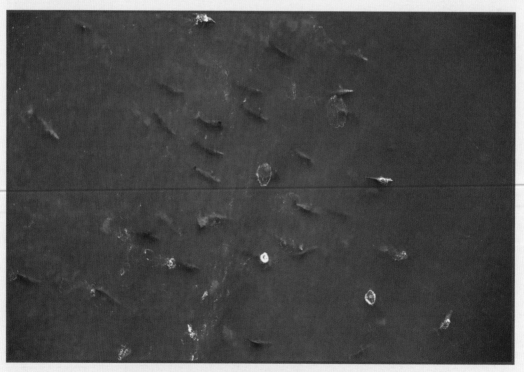

*Unlike most other whales, gray whales usually swim close
to shore. This group swims off of the coast of Mexico.*

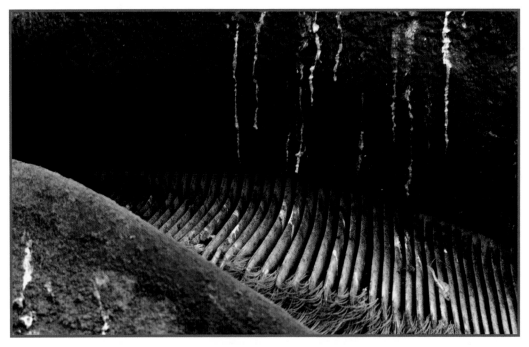

A gray whale's baleen filters out sand and mud like a comb.

Adults are up to 50 feet (15 meters) in length. They can weigh as much

as 40 tons (36,287 kilograms). The animals are named for their mottled

gray skin.

These whales have no teeth. Instead, they have plates of baleen hanging

from the roof of the mouth. Baleen is a stiff, bendable material, much like

Gray whales move through the water by moving their enormous tail fins, or flukes.

plastic, with fine hairs along its edge. The baleen plates form a huge comb that acts like a filter when the whale eats.

To feed, a gray whale dives to the seafloor. It rolls over onto its side and opens its huge mouth. All sorts of things wash in—worms, amphipods, fish, crabs, water, and sand. The whale then forces water out through its baleen plates. Sand washes out with it, but food stays behind, stuck in the baleen comb. The whale swallows everything. Then it scoots forward and opens its mouth again.

A gray whale has a paddle-shaped flipper on each side of its body just behind the head. Instead of a dorsal fin, it has one large hump on its back. Behind this is a ridge of smaller bumps called knuckles.

A whale's tail fins are called flukes. A whale propels itself through the water by pumping its flukes up and down.

Gray whales are outstanding travelers. Every year, they make an incredible journey of more than 10,000 miles (16,090 kilometers). They spend their summers feeding near Alaska. In late fall, they head south.

Learning & Innovation Skills

Like other mammals, gray whales have hair on their bodies. It's on the upper jaw. The whale has many dimples. A single stiff hair grows in each one. What purpose do you think these hairs might serve for the gray whale?

A gray whale calf swims next to its mother, who provides the calf with milk for its first eight months.

The gray whales take about two months to swim to Baja California,

Mexico. This is where they spend the winter. There, in shallow waters,

they nurse their babies, or calves. Some calves are born in the lagoons, but many are born before getting there, during the long journey southward.

A gray whale calf is truly a big baby. A newborn is longer than a pickup truck. It weighs as much as 1,500 pounds (680 kilograms). Calves spend their first few months nursing and gaining weight. They are building up a layer of fat called blubber. Babies will need their blubber to keep warm when they travel to Alaska with their mothers.

In the spring, the whales move north again. They take about three months to reach their Alaskan feeding grounds. During their trips, they rarely swim far from the shore.

Learning & Innovation Skills

Gray whales belong to a group of animals called cetaceans. The group also includes porpoises, dolphins, and other whales. All cetaceans live in water and breathe air. They also nurse their young.

Cetaceans are divided into two groups—toothed whales and baleen whales. Toothed whales have teeth and breathe through a single opening on the top of their head called a blowhole. Baleen whales have baleen and two blowholes. Gray whales are baleen whales. Can you figure out which group dolphins and porpoises are a part of? What information might help you decide?

As it travels, a gray whale comes to the surface from time to time. It

may come up to breathe or to breach. A gray whale breathes through two

A gray whale spy-hopping is similar to humans treading water.

openings, or blowholes, on the top of its head. A whale breaches by leaping out of the water. Then it falls back, making a huge splash.

Spy-hopping is another interesting behavior. When a whale spy-hops, it pokes its head above the surface. It slowly looks around, then goes under again. This may be one way the whale keeps track of its surroundings.

Learning & Innovation Skills

Whales breathe only through their blowholes. They cannot breathe through their mouths. Unlike humans, their mouths are not connected to the windpipe. Only the blowholes are connected to the windpipe, which leads to the lungs. Why do you think the whales have blowholes on the top of their heads?

CHAPTER THREE

A SAD TALE

Today, nearly 20,000 gray whales live near North America. They travel as a group between Mexico and Alaska each year. But in the past, they nearly disappeared.

The Pacific Ocean is home to thousands of gray whales, including this breaching gray.

In the past, hunters on whaling ships like this abandoned boat in the South Atlantic Ocean killed off many gray whales.

At one time, there were actually three gray whale populations. The

third group lived in the Atlantic Ocean. But that population died out in

the 1600s, probably because of whaling.

This engraving from the 1800s shows a successful whale hunt. The dead whale lies in the water while a smoky fire on the ship boils the whale's blubber.

The population that lives near Korea, Japan, and Russia is endangered, or in danger of dying out. There are only around 100 of them left. This is partly because of overhunting.

The group that lives near North America's west coast is a different story. In the 1800s, whaling nearly destroyed the population. But today, these whales have made a great comeback.

Some 200 years ago, whale hunting was quite common. Ships sailed out from the coasts of North America and many other countries. Whalers chased the animals through storms and high waves.

Some of the larger kinds of whales were worth plenty. Their blubber would produce many barrels of oil. Their baleen could be used in

Learning & Innovation Skills

Whalers thought the grays were good only for their blubber and baleen. However, gray whales are very important to other sea creatures. One look at their skin shows that.

Animals called barnacles live on the gray whale's back. In fact, some whales are covered with them. Barnacles are soft-bodied creatures that live in hard shells. Early in life, they glue their shells to something solid like boats, rocks, or whales.

As the whales swim along, water sweeps past the barnacles. The barnacles gather tiny pieces of food from this water in addition to dead skin that may flake off the whale. So the whales also help the barnacles eat. What things in the natural world does the gray whale depend on for survival?

Gray whales are among the largest animals on Earth. Yet they feed on some of the smallest animals around—amphipods. Amphipods are little, shrimplike animals. One amphipod could easily fit on a penny.

Gray whales eat amphipods that live on the bottom of the ocean. Scientists worry that changes in the amphipod habitat could put gray whales back on the endangered species list. For example, how would an oil spill on the ocean's floor affect gray whales?

household items. People bought the oil to burn in their lamps. They used baleen to make the firm support in fans and umbrellas.

Gray whales were easy targets. They stayed closer to shore than other whales. They swam into shallow waters to have their young. It was in these shallow areas that they were easy to find. There hunters waited until the whales came up for air. Then they shot the animals or harpooned them. Hunters harpoon whales by shooting them with a spear attached to a rope.

In deep water, the whales might have escaped. But in shallow lagoons, they had

A gray whale blows air out through its blowholes. Gray whales are easy targets when they come up for air.

nowhere to go. Trapped and dying whales thrashed wildly. Mothers fiercely

protected their young.

Sometimes whalers were killed in all the violence. People began to say

the gray whales were "devil fish." Still, the grays were easier to find than other whales.

By the late 1800s, thousands of gray whales had been killed. Years earlier, there had been around 30,000 grays. Before the hunting stopped, there may have been only 1,000. The gray whales were in serious trouble. They had become an endangered species.

CHAPTER FOUR

THINGS TURN AROUND

In 1937, people finally decided that gray whales needed protection.

That year, several countries agreed to limit whale hunting. In 1947, the

International Whaling Commission spoke out. This group made it against

the law to hunt gray whales. That's when things began to change.

*In 1947, gray whales in the North Pacific Ocean gained complete
protection from the International Whaling Commission.*

Gray whale numbers slowly began to rise. By 1979, there were around 15,000 grays. Ten years later, there were about 20,000. In 1994, the North American population of gray whales made the news. It was announced that they were no longer endangered.

Marine biologists keep track of gray whale populations. These scientists in Mexico's San Ignacio Lagoon use special instruments to monitor a gray whale's heartbeat.

Gray whales prefer to swim near the coastline. But in some areas where the shallow shelf waters extend offshore, they swim too far out to be seen from land. It's hard to know exactly how many grays there are. But since 1967 scientists have been counting grays from the same site in California, where the whales travel close to shore. These counts show gray whales have recovered to a population size close to when hunting began in the 1600s.

In fact, there are so many gray whales that having enough food can be difficult for them. Sometimes their numbers drop when their food decreases.

21st Century Content

Every year, cities in western Canada hold the Pacific Rim Whale Festival. People come to watch the gray whales that are passing through. If they are lucky, they also see humpback and killer whales.

Although the grays are protected, some hunting still takes place. A few native tribes in Siberia and Washington State have special permission to hunt the animal. These tribes have depended on gray whales for hundreds of years. The whales provide food and oil for them.

The Chukchi people of northeastern Russia still hunt gray whales as part of their cultural past and for survival.

CHAPTER FIVE

GRAY WHALES TODAY

Getting caught in a fishing net can mean death for whales.

Although things are improving for the gray whales of North America,

problems still exist. Sometimes the whales become entangled in fishing

lines. They cannot come up for air, and then they die.

Also, as the whales increase, more people want to see them. A growing number of tourists go out in boats to be with them. It is hard to know if these boat tours disturb gray whales trying to feed, mate, or nurse their calves.

The effect of tourism on the gray whale population, especially mothers and their calves, isn't known.

A gray whale spouts and flips its tail as a pelican on a rock looks on and a boat sails by in Baja California, Mexico. Gray whales and humans can live peacefully side by side.

From time to time, their habitat is threatened. In

the 1990s, this happened in Baja California, Mexico.

A company wanted to build a factory there to extract

Gray whales have great friends in the American Cetacean Society. This group began in 1967 with just a few volunteers. Today, the society is much larger. Its members teach thousands of people about whales every year. Some take schoolchildren out on whale-watching trips. Others lead trips to Mexico to see gray whales and their newborns. By sharing their interest in gray whales, these volunteers inspire others to take responsibility for the survival of the species.

salt from the lagoons. It was right where many of the whales come to give birth and nurse their calves. Many people were upset because factories sometimes have accidents and spill poison into the water.

Concerned citizens wanted to protect the whales. They worked hard to keep the factory from being built, and in 2000, they won.

The work is not over, however. The gray whales will always need protection if they are to survive in our coastal waters.

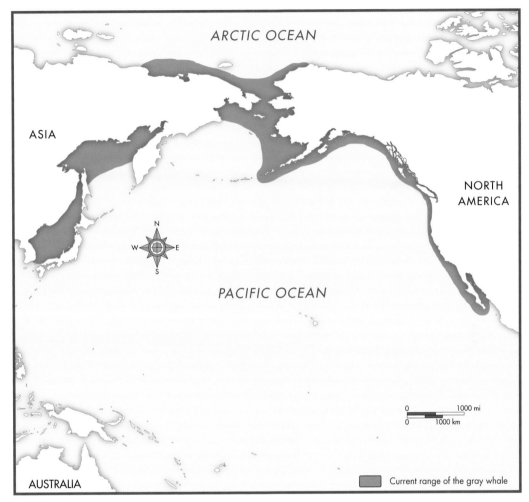

ARCTIC OCEAN

ASIA

NORTH
AMERICA

PACIFIC OCEAN

N
W   E
S

0   1000 mi
0   1000 km

AUSTRALIA

Current range of the gray whale

This map shows the coastal waters where gray whales live.

GLOSSARY

amphipods (AM-fih-podz) small, hard-shelled animals that live in water

baleen (buh-LEEN) stiff, bendable material that hangs in strips from the upper jaw of some whales

barnacles (BAR-nuh-kuhlz) soft-bodied animals that live in a hard shell

breach (BREECH) to leap out of the water

cetaceans (sih-TAY-shuhnz) a group of marine animals that includes dolphins, porpoises, and whales; they all breathe through blowholes

dorsal (DORE-suhl) on the back, such as a fin

endangered (en-DAYN-jurd) in danger of dying out completely

habitat (HAB-ih-tat) the natural home of a plant or animal

lagoons (luh-GOONZ) shallow pools connected to the ocean

mammals (MAM-uhlz) animals that have hair or fur and feed mother's milk to their young

species (SPEE-sheez) a group of similar plants or animals

whaling (WAY-ling) the hunting and killing of whales

FOR MORE INFORMATION

Books

Arnold, Caroline, and Richard Hewett. *Baby Whale Rescue: The True Story of J. J.* Mahwah, NJ: Bridgewater Books, 1999.

Becker, John. *Gray Whales*. Farmington Hills, MI: KidHaven Press, 2004.

Simon, Seymour. *Whales*. New York: Collins, 2006.

Web Sites

Doheny State Beach Interpretive Association—Nature Notes
www.dohenystatebeach.com/nn-whale.htm
For a detailed profile of the gray whale

Gray Whale Watching in Big Sur, California
www.bigsurcalifornia.org/whalesgray.html
For information on gray whale watching in Big Sur, California

Gray Whale—Kids' Planet
www.kidsplanet.org/factsheets/gray_whale.html
To read a fact sheet compiled by Defenders of Wildlife

INDEX

ABOUT THE AUTHOR

Susan H. Gray has a master's degree in zoology. She has written more than 70 science and reference books for children and especially loves writing about animals. Gray also likes to garden and play the piano. She lives in Cabot, Arkansas, with her husband, Michael, and many pets.